Where Is It?

Christine Lindop

Name _____

Age _____

Class _____

OXFORD
UNIVERSITY PRESS

OXFORD

UNIVERSITY PRESS

Great Clarendon Street, Oxford OX2 6DP

Oxford University Press is a department of the University of Oxford.
It furthers the University's objective of excellence in research, scholarship,
and education by publishing worldwide in

Oxford New York

Auckland Bangkok Buenos Aires Cape Town Chennai
Dar es Salaam Delhi Hong Kong Istanbul Karachi Kolkata
Kuala Lumpur Madrid Melbourne Mexico City Mumbai
Nairobi São Paulo Shanghai Taipei Tokyo Toronto

OXFORD and OXFORD ENGLISH are registered trade marks of
Oxford University Press in the UK and in certain other countries

Any websites referred to in this publication are in the public domain and
their addresses are provided by Oxford University Press for information only.
Oxford University Press disclaims any responsibility for the content

ISBN: 978 0 19 440084 8

Printed in China

Illustrations by: Cathy Hughes/Beehive Illustrations

With thanks to Sally Spray for her contribution to this series

Reading Dolphins
Notes for teachers & parents

📖 Using the book

1 Begin by looking at the first story page (page 2). Look at the picture and ask questions about it. Then read the story text under the picture with your students. Use section 1 of the CD for this if possible.

2 Teach and check the understanding of any new vocabulary. Note that some of the words are in the **Picture Dictionary** at the back of the book.

3 Now look at the activities on the right-hand page. Show the example to the students and instruct them to complete the activities. This may be done individually, in pairs, or as a class.

4 Do the same for the remaining pages of the book.

5 Retell the whole story more quickly, reinforcing the new vocabulary. Sections 2 and 3 of the CD can help with this.

6 If possible, listen to the expanded story (section 4 of the CD). The students should follow in their books.

7 When the book is finished, use the **Picture Dictionary** to check that students understand and remember new vocabulary. Section 5 of the CD can help with this.

💿 Using the CD

The CD contains five sections.

1 The story told slowly, with pauses. Use this during the first reading. It may also be used for "Listen and repeat" activities at any point.

2 The story told at normal speed. This should be used once the students have read the book for the first time.

3 The story chanted. Students may want to chant along with the story.

4 The expanded story. The story is told in a longer version. This will help the students understand English when it is spoken faster, as they will now know the story and the vocabulary.

5 Vocabulary. Each word in the **Picture Dictionary** is spoken and then used in a simple sentence.

Where is my lion?

Look, John.

It is under the chair.

OK. I see it.

Number.

lion | 3 | dog |
chair | | cat |
dinosaur | | elephant |

Where is my kitten?

Here he is, Alice.

He is in the tree.

Oh, no. Come down.

1 Number.

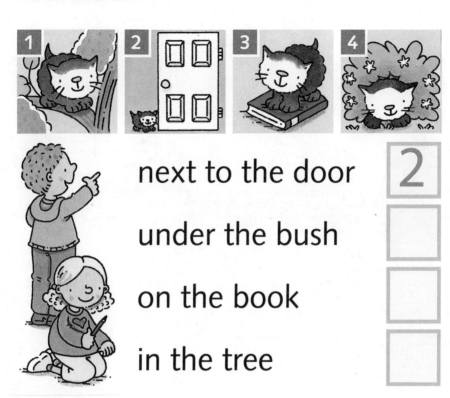

next to the door `2`

under the bush

on the book

in the tree

2 Trace.

in   next to

on   under

Where are my pens?
They are on the desk.
Thank you, Alice.

Connect.

1   in   2

3   on   4

5   under   6

7   next to   8

7

Where is my bag?

It is over here, Granny.
It is next to the door.

Circle.

❶ The book is **in** / (**on**) the table.

❷ The cat is **on** / **under** the chair.

❸ The fish is **in** / **on** the bowl.

❹ The dog is **next to** / **on** the chair.

❺ The ball is **on** / **under** the table.

Where are the eggs?
They are in the box.
Thank you, John.

Connect.

1 • in the fridge

2 • in the bowl

3 • in the box

4 • under the clock

5 • on the fridge

6 • in the fridge

Where are my keys?

Look, Mom.
They are over there.
They are on the TV.

Circle yes or no .

1. Are the keys on the TV?

   yes (circled)
   no

2. Is the pen on the TV?

   yes
   no

3. Is the dog under the TV?

   yes
   no

4. Is the dog next to the chair?

   yes
   no

5. Is the dinosaur under the table?

   yes
   no

6. Are the flowers under the table?

   yes
   no

Where is my hat?
Look, baby. Your hat is
on your head.

Look back through the story. What page?

1. The bag is next to the door. page  8

2. The pens are on the desk. page

3. The lion is under the chair. page

4. The keys are on the TV. page

5. The kitten is in the tree. page

6. The eggs are in the box. page

Picture Dictionary

bag

desk

bowl

dinosaur

box

dog

clock

door

egg

key

elephant

kitten

fish

lion

flower

tomato

hat

tree

Dolphin Readers

Dolphin Readers are available at five levels, from Starter to 4.

The Dolphins series covers four major themes:

Grammar, Living Together, The World Around Us, Science and Nature.

For each theme, there are two titles at every level.

Activity Books are available for all Dolphins.

All Dolphins are available on audio CD.
(2 TITLES ON EACH CD ⬤ SEE TABLE BELOW)

Teacher's Notes are available at **www.oup.com/elt/dolphins**

	Grammar	Living Together	The World Around Us	Science and Nature
Starter	• Silly Squirrel • Monkeying Around	• My Family • A Day with Baby	• Doctor, Doctor • Moving House	• A Game of Shapes • Baby Animals
Level 1	• Meet Molly • Where Is It?	• Little Helpers • Jack the Hero	• On Safari • Lost Kitten	• Number Magic • How's the Weather?
Level 2	• Double Trouble • Super Sam	• Candy for Breakfast • Lost!	• A Visit to the City • Matt's Mistake	• Numbers, Numbers Everywhere • Circles and Squares
Level 3	• Students in Space • What Did You Do Yesterday?	• New Girl in School • Uncle Jerry's Great Idea	• Just Like Mine • Wonderful Wild Animals	• Things That Fly • Let's Go to the Rainforest
Level 4	• The Tough Task • Yesterday, Today and Tomorrow	• We Won the Cup • Up and Down	• Where People Live • City Girl, Country Boy	• In the Ocean • Go, Gorillas, Go